VICTIMS OF A FAILED CIVICS

KEN POYNER

Copyright © 2016 by Ken Poyner

ISBN-13: 978-0692775219
ISBN-10: 0692775218

Front photograph: Steinar La Engeland

Back photograph: Karen Poyner

Book formatting by www.ebooklaunch.com

Barking Moose Press
www.barkingmoosepress.com

Grateful acknowledgement is made to the following publications in which many of these collected pieces first appeared:

Alabama Literary Review

Alaska Quarterly Review

Altadena Review

Antietam Review

Black Fly Review

Blue Unicorn

Calliope

Cincinnati Poetry Review

Colorado-North Review

G.W. Review

Iowa Review

Jam To-Day

Kansas Quarterly

Lodestar

New Mexico Humanities Review

Newsletter Inago

On Stage

Panhandler

Penny Dreadful

Poet Lore

Proof Rock

West Branch

Yarrow

Additionally, some of these pieces have appeared in the following chapbooks:

Cordwood, 22 Press, 1985

Sciences, Social, Palanquin Press, 1995

I

THE BURNING OF THE BARN

The barn at last is finished burning.
People who have come to do
The damned little they could do
Are counting fingers, thinking
Of washing the smoke from clothes,
The smell of damp straw afire
From their hair. Men look over
The backs of their sleeves to make sure
In the effort they haven't ripped a shirt.
Children are out in the field rounding up
The last of the animals. The youngest woman present,
A bride not more than six months,
Is the last to walk out of the house with water.
No one takes the glass she carries.
A man with boots older and more useless
Than those worn by anyone else
Walks into the ash, sees for himself
That fire, given the barn an hour ago,
Will not want the backyard as well,
Will not think of needing the house.
Still in his nightshirt and yesterday's pants,
The man whose barn has come down
Brings out the only two bottles of bourbon he owns,
The flask of rum he has borrowed from the nearest neighbor.
His wife inside is cooking, the stove
Pushed to as hot as it will go: coffee
For the women, biscuits for the men.
Rain for tomorrow.

THE NEIGHBOR OF THE SEMI-RETIRED PSYCHOANALYST

He doesn't think it is a good idea to pry
Into people's dreams. All the popular literature
And late night movies might give it high marks,
But trying to turn a person inside out, and for pay
At that, still seems, to him, a bit left-handed.
Not that he'll make any less of a good neighbor.
Both he and his wife will go over just after
The last of the hired movers drives off,
Bring their own pot of coffee and enough rolls
For conversation, dinner, and to fry tomorrow morning.
He will talk about the soil as though
The man who bought the land intended
To grow anything by design on it. Phone numbers
Will be exchanged, the names of children,
Gossip about the strip of road near the county
Package store, and skeletal information about what families
Can be counted on to do what the community
Has for years assumed to be their sum purpose.
He will tell his wife that he really doesn't mind
As long as the man practices in the city,
And no one for miles has the spare change to put into it.
But still, for weeks, his dreams will have a shell about them;
And even with them being straight lined and without
Language, he will worry somehow they will leak out,
The neighbor will get hold of a corner and pull
Until the last fifty years unravel. He might try
To put himself into a mind for black, thoughtless sleep -
But his dreams will come back yellow and naked
And maybe twice in a week he will wake his wife

To put to good use the energy left from them.
She will be thinking why couldn't the neighbor
Have moved in thirty years earlier, and why
Can't he move away now.

LEG-HOLD TRAP

He howled near two hours before anyone found him.
Serves him right. The land for miles
At waterside is half under-burrowed,
And a pelt will bring a dollar seventy-five.
Besides, put in collards or lettuce
And they'll gnaw the seedlings flat to ground.
Half-drunk he was, until the leg-hold snapped shut,
And then he came up sober pretty damn quick.
A bit of sense and he could have freed himself,
But as it is he's only a little hoarse, the bone
Has a clean break, and the cast will keep him
Away from the McClellan girl long enough
For somebody else to move in. The story
Will keep small children careful for weeks, and away
From the marsh for days. Two weeks,
Two dozen signatures on the plaster, even to
The man on crutches it will be a hell of a fine joke.
I sit by the dock, watching muskrats race the water,
Muskrats that would have my yard full of holes
Were it not for the depth of my new-car expensive bulk-heading -
Their geometrically pure wakes, their sense
Of going somewhere on purpose, their twistless
Twists around weed and dives that are falling without noise -
Ease in the doing, a home in the act, more grace
Than in my best dreams of the best women I can dream.
I'd shoot them from the bank if it weren't for ricochets.

MCCLELLAN SHOOTS HIS DOGS

I heard them singing. Had we slept
With the window closed I'd
Have missed it. Having no time
To dress or even find at the back of the closet
My robe, I threw the covers across you
And made for the back door. Twice
Crossing the yard I stepped in animal droppings,
Stubbed my toe on one of the child's blocks.
I heard them singing. Turning the barn,
At the fence I saw all four of them,
Smallest to large, lined on the lowest rail,
Their mouths guilty with the act.

You said the siren had just gone by,
The fence the boundary nearest the noise.
I could have dreamed the most of it,
Rushed out still half asleep, put
The actual together with the imaginary
And out of such genetics come up
With occurrences rational to explain only what
There never was. I remember shivering
In the morning not quite six o'clock,
My four dogs lined on the rail, excrement
Between my toes and I trying to cover my nakedness.
And then you behind me in a housecoat.

AN ABANDONED WOMAN BECOMES THE LOCAL SCANDAL

I see myself with both feet stuck in the marsh,
The tide coming in faster than children out of a school bus.
Anyone nearby who hears a scream thinks it is
A young girl beset by boys who don't know yet
What sex is. I end up standing there
Until the tide reaches its peak only neck high,
Turning glad of the help the water is in holding my body up.
Tide in, tide out, it must be a good sized forever I wait,
Knowing that as long as I don't put my hands in the muck,
And there are no storms to force a surge onto my fists,
I can last as far as my body is willing to be worthwhile.
It is difficult not in slack water times
To put both hands down, reach into the ooze
Shoulder deep. I see myself
Upright, and not as tired as I might be.
Then one day a man with nothing better to do
In a boat passes and before turning back to rescue me
Yells Damn fool, what would you be doing
Out here, all by yourself? And I think,
Even as I thank him luxuriously for pulling me in,
If I had had a boat we might soon be talking
About something other than my shoes that always
Will remain a foot and a half buried in the shallows.

ADDITIONAL HANDS

Three hours and it will be his soul
We are worried about. Now it is
The smell of the sheets, why
Even with the window open there is
No air. Just two weeks ago
If you take his word at the time
He had Sara Johnson out by Henson's barn
And we all wonder if he's going away with something catching:
Something that, if we're not strong,
In half a month the bitch will pass on to us.
At least he makes little noise of it. His parents
By far are the worst, though his sister
In making the supper is as loud
With pots and pans as a woman
Whose husband tries a little sleep after dinner.
It takes two of us to roll him up,
One to pull free the bottom sheet,
And all three to hold him out of the way
As his mother makes up the bed anew.
Bedclothes in constant rounds are washed
And put back down half wet
And I remember all four of us
Two-thirds drunk on a Saturday afternoon
Pulling sheets down from McClellan's line,
Dragging them across grass that should
Six days earlier have been cut, and wadding them
Over the fence and into the dog pen.
Who'd think, after the way we ran,
Even drunk and only half happy to get away,
He'd be in a bare and ordinary three month's time
So goddamned heavy.

COMMON SENSES

The fool's coming across the field, his dog
Hopping the furrows, he battling down last year's
Corn stubble. What of his
Have you borrowed now that he wants back?
I'd think we have enough money
You can buy whatever you need.
The dog gets a little ahead of him,
Turns back, would rather
Be chasing muskrats I'd bet.
Being that man's dog must be hell.
He comes hunched over, bent forward, as though passing
Through water. When he reaches
The green flatland of our yard
He slows, the dog runs farther ahead,
Farther back, and I'm sure that dog has some
Elementary belief in the effort wasted,
The joy. What is it this time.
You've borrowed everything but the man's gun,
And could use half of it at best.
His rap at the door is as light as a prowler's
Habitual accident. His poor speech,
Built as though with maul and metal-work hammers -
Friendly, quiet and purpose alone -
Will be as thick on the porch as rain.
I'll be sweeping it off the steps for days,
Finding it tangled in my hair, in your pockets.
We hold our language close to our bodies.
You bring his wheelbarrow from behind the house,
Shout with that idiot mockery of speech,
The false accent and loss of vocabulary

You haul out like war material for him,
For all the life-long residents we meet hereabouts.
I play with the dog, pointing at
Trash in the water twenty yards off-shore.
Between the man and you the pidgin language is enough.
When he stops by and you're not home
He says he loves the way I talk.
Like his dog I know what he wants by tone.
We'll clean his butchery of words out of our clothes
With ammonia bleach, wet down the stoop
With hot water and soda. I hear that dog howling,
His almost chemical, unapproachable thoughts turned to noise,
And I wish you'd shut up long enough to listen.

DISCUSSING SEX WITH A SON COMING OF AGE

Some of the pricks of light are not stars,
But galaxies. Other spots
Are clouds where suns are born, ones
That haven't the sense yet to have planets.
Occasionally, a dot is two galaxies colliding,
Suns and worlds of each in the black-eyed emptiness
Passing without notice, entire races
Sliding against one another
Without the damnedest knowledge either of the other.
I'd like to think I'd know if someone else,
Perhaps with fins and a beak and a poetry
Of gas, volume and geometry rather than word, meter and rhyme,
Were going incuriously by. At the edge of the universe
Great blue areas are doing something
No one I know has been let in on. I don't want to know.
I have enough to worry about keeping the rabbits
Out of the garden, and surely someone
With a beak and fins has something
Too cute to kill that makes a mess of what
All of a thirty-six hour day he's been doing.
Falling stars are just hunks of unattached rock
And a comet is ice that howls for being too close to the sun.
I hear Ellen Sue McClellan has been known to put out,
If you're lucky, and approach her just right.

DECREASING THE SNAKE POPULATION

The head half an inch just out of water.
Or the whole length
Supported by a tangle of water grass,
Dark ripple at the surface. After years
Of rocks, slingshots with marbles,
The boys now have twenty-twos, are cautioned
About the ricochet of a small caliber from water.
A moving S is the prized shot.
A snake at shore is almost too easy.
Better to scare it out, move it
Ten feet into the Sound,
Nip the head at the water line.
Snakes are not always plentiful.
The boys have knocked dragonflies out of the air.
Their fathers are cautious men, who have
Threatened that with too much recklessness
The rifles will be locked a good time
In the land of rust and corrosion
That is the metal shed out back. A toad
Or squirrel, or one of the crows that no longer
For a man cutting a yard on Sunday morning
Is one too many. The shells are within
A frugal boy's allowance, and one father
Owns a reloader where the casings can be packed
To half again their original strength.

A dog that does not know his best
Friends. Independent cats. The rabbits
That have become rare of late. The younger boys
Are all so small, and the girls with one shell

In the chamber more like sex.
By McClellan's fields the boys cross the woods
Holding their rifles out of the stubble:
Rangers as real as last night's movie and without
A good enemy, as up ahead the bushes
Are not still. They can feel, all around,
The beginnings of snake thoughts.

MOYOCK DISCOVERS IT IS LESS THAN AN HOUR AWAY FROM THE WORLD'S LARGEST NAVAL BASE, AND A POTENTIAL TERRORIST TARGET

We dream of the man who one day,
For no good reason, will stoop beside our water supply
And let into our world the wiggling death
He has in a basement sink at home concocted.
Or the woman who will burst into the supermarket
With a machine gun that costs two week's pay
And spray lead into a housewife or two,
A school boy bagging groceries, the Johnson's
Recent success after six years of infertility.
A bomb parked outside the courthouse.
Gas, nerve or mustard, rigged to spray
From the back of a pickup truck, with shell,
By way of a contraption that could win even a larger town's
All-school science fair. House to house,
The wires down, for the most basic of plots
We would be easy targets. A man
With a shotgun, and even a son of age,
Is no match for someone who worships
A left handed god. The community unanimously
Passes a resolution. We gather less often
In large numbers. We keep our personal itineraries
To ourselves. We learn to breathe
Through handkerchiefs, boil water,
Treat wounded. We listen to the edited war stories
Of those amongst us old enough to have done

Their editing well. Our children will grow up.
Fishermen bring in suspicious trash that has been dumped
Near the public boat slips. Good men
Stop molesting their nieces. The church
Is more close to filled than any time since legalized abortions.
And we read the paper.

You'd be surprised what they put in there.

MCCLELLAN'S AMERICA

The wife I've set to taking down the fence.
The littlest girl rolls the screens, ties them
With shreds of curtain. Both boys
And a neighbor dismantle the first of the barn,
Number code it, load it flat on the truck.
Our chickens run about behind the house
As the front stoop is sawn to three pieces,
Packed in the trunk. Window sills
Are strapped to the hood of the car.
Barbed wire, by rolling down the glass,
We've strung across the sedan's roof,
Yard after yard wound inside the cab to out.
Most of the concrete we cannot carry.
A deep pipe or two will not go.
Porcelain fixtures have been boxed, stacked
In the backseat. Window frames and doorjambs
Are strung to the bed of the truck; house siding
Leans too far over the tail
And another method may need be found.
The outhouse, once so much an importance, we could not
Make a place to store, so it stays.
Already weeds are working at our leftover bricks;
Stalks bent by our home's edges are straightening;
A dog without the ordered fortress of fence,
Barn and house chases a rabbit too far.
Car and two trucks, we move low to the ground,
Overloaded, a boy flinging nails bent in removal
Back into the grass that once was front yard.
Our cow, standing at the line of land-rut
That held the wall of late a quarter of barn,
Thinks *who now will come to me and milk?*

IF SEX IS IMPORTANT TO MARRIAGE

Myrna says she has been raped by aliens.
Asked how it went, she says it was like nothing
Sexual. She didn't even have to get undressed.
Just a tap to her forehead, heat all over,
And she could feel an invading presence
Curl up to home in her womb. Her husband
With three beers in him on Friday night says
That is about how it would have to happen
With Myrna. A cold woman, with a sense
Of duty but no joy in it, her thoughts
On how the most simple of acts should logically proceed
Seem to come from one too many comic book romances
And a belief that sin will leak back to the *National Enquirer*.
Smart alien, he says, to use a tap on the forehead
And save himself hours of work without a measurable end:
About time someone popped some sense into her.
God knows, he doesn't want the task anymore.
But it is his wife, and most likely his child,
And he has noticed sometimes in the middle of his best efforts
She does bend her knees or look down from the ceiling -
And once, half way through, to keep from enjoying herself
She started to recite out loud the week's shopping list.
He leans back in his chair, both hands behind
The six week's scruff collecting on his neck,
Smiles like a man a full six pack further along
And says a tap to the forehead. Must have been
One hell of a potent alien.

ASSIGNMENT

Someday someone's going to put a stake through her heart.
An unmarried woman alone is bad enough.
The talk for a while might be all flat side
Or round, but at the bottom everyone
Would feel better off if she took up
With one of the men from the garage,
Let us put a label on our discontent.
We see her at midnight sitting on her front porch,
Not a light in the house on save the one
Naked by the door behind her.
We'd rather our young boys built their fantasies
Around some other woman twice their age -
But she has the look, and moves sometimes
In the unlicensed way that could scare
A snake out from under a warm front stoop.
I've caught myself watching her, but good looks
And even wearing one's sex much better than most
Is only enough to put us to envy and anger.
Sometimes she stares out of her window
At nothing at all. No one visits.
It is rumored that four of the McClellan boys half drunk
Caught her alone one night at the edge of the Sound
Just by Henson's woods, and had by force
With her as much of their way as they could muster.
About it she has said nothing, but her silence
Draws all of us into the belief, and even
The McClellan boys have ceased to talk of it.
With the wind in her hair everyone
Knows there is more than wind to it.
Some suspect her of having a hidden garden,

Of growing herbs and half sickly plants
To our land unknown before now:
When anyone falls between well and doctor-trip ill
She is adjudged to know chemistries that good people forget.
Only for my wife's sake will I say there is something to it.
As long winded, clumsy and quick to anger
As the McClellan boys have proven in everything else,
The woman is sure to have a fistful of memories
That keep her half a step off line.
But I see nothing to fear, wouldn't myself
Mind spending an hour or two - the wife
Thinking I'm out back with the bones of the chevy -
Inside the dark of that house with her. With one side
Of the hand or the other we surely
Could find ground for a common understanding.

PURPOSE

Put down enough random numbers
And we'll get your waist size.
More, and there will be my age.
Eventually, our bank account number,
Prefix, substance and suffix - though first
The house number, the birth dates
Of our children, the weight in pounds of a ton.
Soon the number of electrons in the outer shell
Of a Manganese atom, the combination ratio
For hydrogen with sulphur and oxygen.
Somewhere in the Veblenesque mass will be
The number of gallons our gas tank holds,
The ohms for speakers, shoe sizes,
Hat sizes, the dress size for the waitress
With the sensuous pixie hair cut at
Davidson's Restaurant, her shoe size,
Her hat size, her waist and hips and bust.
Finally, her complete phone number,
The apartment address, the number of blocks
East and then north from the restaurant,
An hour of meeting. Lines of factory workers,
Pragmatic, meaningless individually, solely ordered
By the moment, unrelated, without reflection.
The length of her legs, the pressures about her mouth.
You let my fantasies too greatly worry you.

NEW SHOES FOR THE FIFTEEN YEAR OLD

I sit cross-legged on the porch
Like the sister we never speak of.
Thirty minutes after the family left
I had my blue dress
Out from under the mattress springs
And was stealing perfume.
Rocking in father's chair
On the front porch by the highway
Dark stockings rip on splinters,
And my make-up runs with July sweat.
The dress wrinkles and goes black.

The truckers don't care.

THE PRODIGY

Understand you are sitting too late in the kitchen
When you begin to notice the dust that for decades
Has hidden at the edge of the cabinets.
Want to wake the wife, complain
Her housekeeping leaves at least this much
To be desired. Know
It comes from sitting too late in the kitchen.
At last the coffeemaker ends its hiss;
Hear coming from the night
The slightest sound of his whistling. From the pitch,
He has moved off the dock, is walking
The bulkhead. Pour the coffee,
Pick up the fray of his music again.
The cat, its paws in the still house
On the linoleum as loud as a child at breakfast,
Peers at you from the worn spot
In front of the refrigerator, turns back
To the dark house. Somewhere up the stairs
And in the last room by the rail - listen
To your wife turn over, feel the buckling of the bed
In your ribs. From outside, the sound
Grows ever less: imagine
He is at the border of your land,
Facing the tangle of brush and reed wild
With birds waiting out the dark, casting
The nadir of his faith - his mouth
Caked, even teeth sore, his lungs
Pulled to slits. Perhaps, back
In the boat slip, writhing in the water
And its own confusion will be the one snake

That all night he has been able to whistle up.
Go out as quietly as you can
With the blanket that each trial for weeks
You've used to gather the exhausted boy in.
Half asleep, he will not know his father from any man.

How beautiful that one snake.

WHY HENSON IS BEATING HIS WIFE

Half the roof went out with the wind
And it is nobody's fault.
Even the tar paper had been tacked down sure.
All day we had waited for rain
And for the wait it came down angry,
With hail in places, and lightning
Over the Sound and waves blown beyond docks.
More than a boy in love with storms
With his dog under a tarp in the backyard
Could stand. An otherwise good roof.
But perhaps with too much eave,
And that at a bad angle. Not simply shingles gone,
But wood flung across the garden,
The fence that was no more than ornament
Knocked over and in places splintered.
Two-by-fours and two-by-sixes and plywood
All with a few days drying to be
The bottom of a fire you lay a better log on.
Squealing, the joists singing, an act
Of God, unnecessary, and at a bad time as well.
Nothing to do but stand in the storm
After the storm, watch the water
Run from even the vertical.
Homeowner's insurance will cover the work,
And what seeps through to the living room,
And refinishing grandmother's desk that needed
Refinishing anyway, and cleaning not only the damp smell
But all the smells out of the carpet, along with
The fleas brought by too many years of too many strays.
But nothing covers the act itself.

MCCLELLAN BURIES THE BONES OF THE MAMMOTH IN HIS BACKYARD FOR SAFEKEEPING

They came out of his front yard
One at a time. Luckily the first
Was good thigh, didn't break,
And jolted his curiosity. He doesn't have
Much of a front yard. When he got
The huge, beautiful bone out,
Washed it down with the garden hose,
He knew he had something maybe,
With a good agent, could be turned
Into money. As he dug them up
Each bone he piled on his side porch
Between his outdoor chair and the swing,
Shielding them from discovery by road
And the casual passerby. Everybody knows
When he gets in these states there is no reason
To ask him what he is doing: he doesn't know,
And couldn't tell what he knows for his energy.
Half a dozen small bones he cut in half,
And a few came apart under the hose;
But his wife praised him, to keep him out of the house,
And he worked on, learning by the tusks
Just what he had. His sense is part way
Between dumping the evidence in the Sound,
And calling the University; we don't criticize:
It keeps him busy. His yard
Looks like a depot shelled, crabgrass
Gaping, more worms than he could fish
A month with, a returnable bottle

Whole turned out now and again,
And a few pounds of metal going bad.
October, and he's stripped down to a T-shirt.
We wonder how he is going to hide the hole,
Until we see him pushing his wheelbarrow
From around the back.

PAS DE

She dances alone, crazy.
Her parents leave her by herself and,
Five minutes after they've driven away,
Every light in the house is on,
Her feet are making a mess of the living room.
She is no trouble. I'd get her to school,
Let the county talk. She'll never
Make a living, but she can learn.
She dances past the kitchen window
And I don't mind sitting on the porch to watch.
Her night shirt beats against flesh
And the light behind her there is very little
My imagination has to fill in.
She moves pointe into the bedroom,
Skips through the pantry and dining room.
I don't think I'd leave a mad girl
Of fifteen alone to roam the place,
Dance herself silly in a house full of light.
We're the closest neighbors and the McClellan boys
Have been frisky of late, have sneaked into
The drive-in and seen the x-rated fare.
Anyone coming by the door would know
She has not wit to see the texture of things.
Her hair whips around and around and she seems
To never get dizzy no matter how long she spins.
I bet there's not a bit of music to it.
You've asked a dozen nights now how often
I'll sit to watch the dancing idiot
Stitching trouble to the light a half mile away.
You hum a little beneath your breath

And in a month I'll have you singing,
Arias, cantatas by the ton jammed in our bedroom
Like wood against the winter, rotting apples.

THE LOVERS IN THE ATTIC

Originally, I could imagine them both lying down
To a simple check and balance, white sheets
And just a little light and the slow of it
Crashing like Sound fog through the marsh.
A few weeks and I thought of them
Now and again getting a little wound up,
Took every thump on the ceiling as the bed
Shifting, or a limb falling and only later
Dragged back into place. Not long and I could see
He would be wearing suede vests,
She dark stay-up stockings. As long as they don't
Make too much noise, scar the walls,
Get the neighbors talking. Ropes, handcuffs,
Leather - whatever, given they are at breakfast
Still civil, meet their obligations by due date.
Their breath at times seems to take
All the air in the house, with me waiting
To see if this time the walls will fall in,
The windows give by like cinders to the vacuum.
An attic so crowded it seems the two of them
Could barely fit, let along get acrobatic;
And at a cost that should have them
Living in their own home, secure,
With a neighbor's boy to cut the grass.
Occasionally, they give up the mattress altogether,
Work on the floor above my head
Like snakes in clutch, or sometimes dogs, killing.
What they will be into next I haven't the courage
To explain to my wife. But I picture them
Beyond the dexterity I had even at my best

And tell the wife just possibly, with will
And a reason to, two people
Could fit in the attic, if they lie close,
And I take the insulation out.

THE SEARCH

Somewhere there is a girl out there.
Not dressed for nights this time of year
She can't get far before the limbs
Go numb, and we with our warmth catch up.
The idea
Is not to pass her. She could go
For a tree, or could have put herself already
Into the Sound, be floating face down in the reeds.
A girl could pick a better night to do herself in.
Summer, when a pleasant day doesn't turn
Into drizzle and a north sounding breeze.
I'll kill her damn boyfriend, or whoever it was
Pushed her to this. I have
My own to tend to. A good looking girl,
Not safe in these woods where the hunters
From closer into the city come to get drunk
And spotlight deer, shoot road signs and occasionally
Porch lights. If she wasn't bent
On killing herself someone might do it for her
After a while. There are so many options
When a girl has legs like that
And a walk that goes a long way.
I've watched her myself. I'm not sure
That half the men out here tonight
Finding her alive but uncaring might
Be tempted. None of them the type
To do anything truly by force, but maybe
Without asking, if the resistance is weak.
Nobody spends that much time in the woods anymore.
Even in daylight we would be confused.

The idea
Is to focus on her mother, fisting the porch
With the note, saying why
Would my little girl do this.
My little girl. A smile
As though she owned all of the world's teeth.
A form that even last summer didn't need
To grow into a woman's bathing suit. The idea
Is to stay within shouting distance,
Each man able to see the next man's light,
To let nothing pass between us,
To be sure of ourselves.

THE WOLF

Ordinary people shut their windows
And, even when there is a breeze, rely on air conditioning.
Screened in porches are left vacant.
Johnson has let loose his wolf again.
When it was fresh from the northwest
Children would hold it to their necks,
Passing child to animal, animal to child,
The speed of the blood. Now, almost
One hundred pounds, Johnson lets it out at night.
His garden is still eaten by rabbits
But boys dare each other in groups of three
To wait at the edge of the marsh
Where last week footprints of some kind were found.
Grown men talk of seeing it in their yards,
Of not being able to get off a clear shot.
In daylight Johnson brings his beast
To Henson's store, where it sprawls flat on the porch,
With Henson scratching it behind the ear
And ladies in house cleaning clothes
Dodging its happy but lethargic tail.
In the dark it has no collar. It loves
The corners of houses, the backs
Of metal sheds bought prefab from Sears.
One man saw it by midnight eating a cat.
Wolves do their damage in packs, do not
Have members named Charlie. But McClellan
Has seen something huge and amber pass by
His locked downstairs windows, and from
The second story, his head halfway out into the night,
Has called to it, lonely and rising at the end,
And thought something prowling near
Was moved to think about him.

THE WOODS OFF ANY NEAR COUNTRY ROAD

Your feet here make something of themselves.
Bottles, beer cans, cigarette wrappings:
They owe an allegiance. Brush,
Gathered twigs, fern, pine branches
Hold everything a man might need
To be a man: the material backs up.
You wear your firm bottomed tennis shoes
To protect yourself from pop tops, small shatters
Of glass. Farther on there are newspapers.
Someone has set up a chair - an old
Heavily cushioned beast, with an ashtray
On the arm, a box turned up
To be a footstool. Cigarette butts
Are dense in the soil; cautiously,
Over years, they come apart and are lost.
More often you see rusted things - coagulations
Of metal, discarded machines. Now,
Hundreds of yards from the road, deep
Into no place, you are finding skeletons
Tied to trees, torn dresses, widowed stockings. The wind
Drives shreds of cloth along occasional spots
Worn flat, pounded almost into gravel.
Yard by yard you work forward,
The brush growing thicker. Much deeper
There is a car. No glass, no mirrors,
No bumpers, no tires, no doors, the corpse
Rots quietly against the ground - ripped seats,
A house of passion, a delight and
A violence. You give the creature plenty of room.

Up ahead there is a channel of sun
And straining you see another road.

Running awkwardly on all fours you get across.
On this side you remember never to look at anything whole:
To hide low against the land,
To look at the pieces, the pieces.

TRUST

You can sell the man anything. Convince him
One day it will be rare, one day
It will be valuable. Tell him
All the girls soon enough will be standing
Naked in line to see one. He drives prices
Up. He buys day old bread with fresh bread money
And is thoughtful for it. He is
About two pints short of a quart.
But he is better known than any man for miles,
And all the neighbors do come over
To stumble through his house-filling collection
Of the useless and the overstocked and the simply
Old and broken. He stands on his porch
Waving good-bye, wearing his buck and a quarter
Idiot's grin, with one of his huge, working-man's hands
Alive like a cough in his pocket.
Please do come back. They remember him
At Christmas. And even if they laugh
They wave, tell their children he does no harm.

THE TRAVELING SALESMAN

Cinderblock foundations.
Flower gardens in front, vegetable gardens
In back. Single pole clotheslines.
White, and in need of painting.
The dump by long standing agreement
Two hundred yards down, and to the left.
Three men with three ideas and no more
Working on one car. A house
With Kentucky fescue, the remainder with crab grass.
One yard with two wind figures.
Children out in the woods. Cats.
Windows open, screens removed. Electric fans,
Huge and bolted into place. Wood frame doors,
With the wire in them ripped, and replaced
Once in a decade. Springs which pull
Hinges out of place, give the land its wonderful
Slap and haunting vibration. Time
Revolving around lunch and dinner. Breakfast
Is what you get when you get up on time.
All the world melted to one pregnant girl
Standing shy in a doorway, waiting for her parents,
Waiting for the heavily named stray dog
To come home. I will do well here.

II

PRACTICALITY

The temperance leaguers have yet to hit this town.
The saloon does a lively business, sheds light
On a porch full of bodies. The mayor
Is known to like a nip or two. The cathouse
Has its own bar, stocks it by the gallon.
Small boys are given wine occasionally at mealtimes;
No one would think it a crime. Most people
Believe the large, mannishly built women
With their hand axes are making a public revenge
For personal disabilities. Young girls
Are given beer on the street corner and not a few
Have been by it compromised into a youthful pregnancy.
A man can bring his bottle into any restaurant,
Go about his business until he passes out.
All around, the towns here have been taken,
Bars hacked to kindling, glass broken,
Billiard tables ripped. Our pastor
Reads from the Bible, passes out naked
In his front yard. Drunken schoolboys
Walk arm in arm along main street
And once again someone has set fire
Accidentally to the trash in an alleyway.
I'd not be surprised if tonight - the firemen
Laid up in the firehouse, alcoholic singing
Raging all along the place - half a block
Didn't smolder before it put itself out.
One night the whole place will burn down,
Or the garbage backing up will run us out,
Or the sloth in town services will produce disease.
The temperance leaguers don't come here.

Poor son-of-a-bitch, the police chief
Unable to stand crawled under a wagon to sleep
And the wagon owner in a bourbon fit
Taking off caused the wagon wheel to stave in
The police chief's head. Out in the hills
The temperance leaguers are camping, keeping watch,
Waiting to see if we will give in.
I wave my half empty bottle at the wilderness:
I'll not be the one to bring them offers of peace,
To stumble through the woods, pants
Fouled at my ankles, hold out my hands in surrender.

THE DIVORCE

When he came into the yard you locked
The doors, closed the window, put out
The fire and I wondered why. The man
Is sixty feet tall, unnumbered tons -
If it is us he is after, he'll rip off the roof:
To crush the house he only needs step; yet
I doubt he wants even our stock to eat.
Coming in he knocked over a fence, but no matter.
Clumsiness is not malice. Too often
You worry there be no good in anything you fail
To hold in hand. Take the better of it:
The hilding is in our yard, I can't make him move,
The ground is not much worse for his shoes,
I'll not let it keep me from collecting the eggs.
Now I only worry that you, bent double,
Crouched with back against the living room ceiling,
Will not stop short of tearing the house in half,
Of forcing the roof off its joists.
If only you could stop growing larger by the minute
All three of us might have peace.

HOW THE SMALL COMMUNITY DEALS WITH THE BIRDMASTER

Morning coffee and all the community
Except Mrs. Johnson up at about the same time.
She stands on her porch arms raised and does
Nothing. Five minutes, ten, she is still
And her thoughts are birds - crows, hawks,
Starlings and jays. For the effort
Nations of birds should settle on her front porch.
Occasionally a crow traveling to breakfast in the field
Will fly over, or a starling prune the yard for seed,
But she has no effect. She goes back in
And all day is as normal as any woman.
We don't ask questions. We no longer
Go to the window to look, or hold up our day
By sitting bedside on the second floor waiting at the pane
For her to go through her morning manipulations.
It is as through anyone else in long-johns
Were to raise the window on winter
And take three breaths. We can be as tolerant
Of the obviously crazy, so long
As what they do is not what we want to do,
As any community with good credit and surpluses.
But we keep our bird feeders well stocked
And let a little of the crop go to crows,
Pay boys to tie tin pans in her bushes,
And feed stray cats at the property line.
Mrs. Johnson gets up and says her power line
Sags more than most, but we never listen to her,
And believe her husband died just for the rest.

MEMORY

A man at the side of the road
Is trying to lift an earthworm
From the gutter. Thin and shallow,
Still the worm stretches itself
Gray in the pool of water, then knots,
As the man tries to touch it
With only two fingers - to hold it
Without cutting it with his nails
Or having to use the clean of his hand.
The rain has only recently stopped.
For eleven hours carefully the water came down.
Drains filled slowly. All day trees will be drying,
Expansion joints in sidewalks bubbling. Nearby
There is a patch of grass.
If a grip can be gotten,
An underhand toss made,
The small unclean thing
Might work its way down,
Through the grass, into too soft soil.
Others begin to watch the man.
He bends less and squats more.
His fingers will not do as they should, as he wants.
With the back of his breath he curses.
It is raining again, lightly.
A woman briefly he does not know
Holds an umbrella over him.

SNOWMEN

One year he set up sixteen,
Good work for his small yard,
And knocked them down in one stiff shouldered run.
The sixteen he had to lay out like a course,
Be sure not to use too much ice -
But most often it was only one, or three,
Or, with children around to be impressed,
Five. That year of sixteen
Neighbors watched, panting fog on their windows,
Smearing glass clean with fingertips or noses,
Watched eight, nine and ten go,
A spray of snow and the busted globes
Of snowmen chests rolling with a limp away -
And still the man's shoulder primed forward:
He running, out of breath, but with the backs
Of his legs, fourteen, fifteen. In retirement
In Florida, he studies the humid winter's
Snow on the Christmas specials, on the cards
Sent by past neighbors. He thinks
Had the snow been less wet, had the city
Not salted the streets so soon, sixteen
Would have been nothing, he would have borrowed
His neighbor's corner lot and gone maybe
For thirty. A boy someplace
Where the snow is drier and the city
Hasn't the salt for backland streets
Builds snowmen six feet high, loves them
A week, sometimes less, as their soft bodies
Melt, run into the yard only to be days later
Built again with another change in weather.

THE REALIST

He could not get enough of it.
Basket upon basket he ate, stuffing
His mouth until his cheeks bulged,
Swallowing as though taking ocean water.
Mirrors were his major source of agriculture.
Often he would scrape the light off raw
And eat it with its designs intact.
Other times he would mash it in a kettle,
Boil it until no particular pattern could be seen.
Cut glass and forceps he forced the matter in,
Incautious in his mastication, brittle
In his digestion. But a short time
And he grew to twice his normal size.
Filled with brilliance he would waddle
From table to window to mirror
And the means of subsistence was all of him.
His belly, bloated with light, hung
Weightless over the arms of his chair.
The man was growing too large with the things
He understood, but the real limit was not
The man - and he ate, eating entire spectacles
Whole. I understand that when
His bursting at last came, the moon
Would not come out all the week. His wife
For days could not remember his name.
The unadulterated brilliance chased children in the streets.
Unknown to him, we have kept a photograph.

UNISON

We're heading out to dig up Abigail.
Statistically, she has been dead thirty-seven years,
Died at fifty-two of an unwound heart
And was put to earth by a mournful husband
Who two years later married a woman
Half his age. No matter.
Of late the rains have not been what we need.
A month ago it was too much rain,
And we dug up George Kimble, put a stake
Through his heart, cut off the head
And finally burned the body for good measure.
Before that it was the aphis, and Christina Lot.
Not that any part of it is a particular disaster,
But this is far better than thinking we have
To wait out the weather, outlast the pests.
No matter what we do no doubt it will turn out all right:
Somehow the species has come this far.
But we keep ourselves busy trying
To make it seem like our troubles
Even minor are somehow supernatural.
So Saturday night, a few beers down and
The younger crowd making a date of it,
We will bring the body up, commit the ritual
And know that in the overall order
We have assigned the blame and settled
The physics of our discomfiture
Together.

WINTER MIGRATION

For some time he has wanted to sit on his porch,
Rock back, and in his hand break a living bird.
The rush of feathers, the pain of feet
Finding on his thumb a perch,
The cavalry of his fingers closing down,
Cage and release. His wife worries he will make the fact,
Will damage his palm, collect rabies,
Bleed on his coveralls, be unable to work.
Small things can lead to lost time. The man
Has thought of solid bone as being more than hollow,
Of hair keeping the body's heat. His nails
Tap the flat of his knee. The veins
In his hand like pipe burst at the skin;
The wife has cautioned a stroke to be next,
A paralysis of one side, or the arm,
Or a loss of nerve. Overhead
Ribbons of bird try the air with pops
And whistles, feathers, excrement and clear direction.
On the porch rail a starling, three jays
Have stopped and a fifth comes to sit
On the boards. The woman watches
Her man's unaltered motion. The grackle
Skips a bent tube chair leg and draws near.
The beak in flesh too short a knife;
The wings a drowned man's coat.
Behind, the woman throws open the screen door,
Traces the thin shriek of flight, is for the moment
Out of danger.

THE GIVER OF GEOMETRY

Trapezoids.
When was the last time he said this to you?
His mouth the yellow flame that burns
Without striations of color
And too close to the wick.
Parallelograms.
The back of the hand.
Fingers too short and the wrist too thin.
Knuckles like stones at the beach.
He said. And then he listened.
Rhombus.
I am not your counting dog.
Not one, not two, not three,
Not four, not five, not six,
Nor seven, eight, nine.
Arctangent.
Smooth. Down the thigh to the knee,
Past the bend. Across the back of the neck
And onto the shoulders. Through the hair.
The hair like a wick in yellow flame.
Hypotenuse.
A long gray cat, longer than any cat
In the world can be, laps at the pool
While the dog counts each flick of the tongue.
Dodecahedron.
In the dark, clear water
He has no business. But he places
The flat of his hand on the bottom
And comes up for air.
Trapezoids.

He said. And nothing more.
You wanted them so terribly
Your body was as flat as glass
And not even your tongue delicious.
You wanted him.

THE LAST AFTERNOON

We have been having sex twice a week
For as long as I can remember.
I see no reason this day should be different.
We're long past what the species needs in our acts;
We are enough our own morphology to do as we like.
To give a little license shows but how,
With measures out of hand, you fall to
The base of our lives and petty hysterias.
I shall be no party. The time each morning
I put aside to work in the garden this morning
Will be spent working in the garden. Economics
Jingoism geopolitics and pounding
Your worn flesh on that rough mattress is not
My concern. Think of how at the first
The thing will be like McClellan's July Fourth fireworks.
Years we have been past the dramatic - on the porch,
Or in the bed. Enjoy the goddamned sight.

THE RIGHTIST

I figure it is a disgrace. No longer
Can we carry the kids over to his house -
And when we go there alone my wife watches me
As though I were a guest thief in her clean kitchen.
I don't see how she keeps a shape, the tank
But four yards long, two deep and two wide.
He buys fish raw in Moyock, keeps them on ice,
Tosses them over the side. She had loved him
Weeks into his last merchant marine trip
Before of her he knew anything. I think
It would have been better had he never
Looked into the water, saw the single green
Fluke, the yellow hair, blue eyes and sea-white skin.
I imagine they must have planned it
On nights while he leaned over the side,
She kept even with the ship at surface.
A passing of whispers. She could have swum
Right into the Sound, been picked out by him
In some kind of hoist, settled into the tank
And rolled to the house. The two of them
Seem as happy as any couple. Her lower body
Nothing but green scale, the scandal is
The upper part they yet refuse to put
In some half a bathing suit - and ballast
She has a magnificence of. The wife all the way home
After evenings we spend in courtesy calls at their house
Talks like a fire dying in elm. The paper boy
There comes to collect three times each week.
She drags our concern across the front of her aquarium
And my spouse is close to vindictiveness.

A conversation because of it the four of us cannot hold;
The gossip in the community cannot go through
Its usual course. One day I go over
With the intention, wifely inspired, of telling him,
Of asking him please to have her put something on,
Let me have a little peace in my home, and he comes to the door
Wrapped in a towel, dripping wet, the carpet
All around the tank in the living room soaked.
His eyes slowly getting their color back, his arms
And legs obviously racked with cramps,
I look past him to the beast crowded against glass
And think for the first time just how small that damn tank is…

LIVING IN THE TROPICS

I have been lucky up to this point.
The snow has fallen at night;
Each dawn I have a new path.
Wolves track the rabbits I scare.
The deer hardly look up when I pass.
I sleep with bear. No one knows
How far I will go. Maps have forgotten me.
The trees are twisted snatches of pine
And the predators starve. I hear water
Beat against ice, the spray crystals hissing
In shore drifts. I leave my shirt on a chair
And wade bare-chested against the wind.
Death is certain: ice crystals form in my mouth.
This season I will not be beguiled.

OKLAHOMA

Even this near to water
The sight of a beached boat terrifies me.
The keel shovel-nosed in sand.
The mast pointing like a dead man's erection.
There is the need to climb into the boat, near the rudder,
To sit with both hands on imaginary ropes,
One's own breath stuck fanatically
In the nonexistent sails.
One may never get back. The tide might not rise,
The gang of fishermen might not return
To haul the boat and its surprise to sea.
Later a man both a girl's dream and nightmare
Might then come along and laugh
At the woman-shape in a pile of salt bone.
Wood holds a pristine boat-likeness
In the air, against sand, as if,
As if the physique of a boat
Were all there were to the shape of a boat.
Let's make a fire.

POLITICAL DISEASE

It would have done well enough
To drive up to the front yard, parked
Open faced in the driveway, done in
The head of household when he answered the door,
Taken out the whole family room by room.
Nobody would have said anything.
For weeks after children would have been
Bursting at each other with sticks, sputtering
Weapons fire with sore tongues and lips
Too wet. The new family in the house
Would have left enough of the stains
So that by moving only a bed or a chair
The violence could be proved. Or the whole group
Somehow could have been gotten into a car, with
An accident concocted—or even a trailing Buick sent,
Overtaking them to conduct business at roadside. Explosives
Bring an extra expense, endanger
The children of families both suspect and not.
Fire, and what furniture can be the night after
Claimed by a man and his older sons
Is charred on three sides, warped, fit only
For a back bedroom. Families from front porches
Stare as the wood burns and good carpet strips bubble black.
The names of the turned-out family are not in months spoken.
A house, and its usable holding, it takes time
And tools to build. Waste angers everyone.

KNOWING WHAT TO DO

The first one he shot was a man
With three days' growth of beard in route
To the barber shop. One report, a single bullet
Somewhere to the midsection. It was then
We noticed the man having the gun. Two boys
Said they had seen him before, noted his old clothes,
That he had been in town for some time.
Black shirt, chaps, dark hat, a four day
Beard. Having noticed him you could not have failed
To notice him. A girl on the sidewalk
He knocked down with a glancing shot off the leg,
Finished with a slug to the back of the head.
Unlike earlier accounts, parts of the face
Were left undistinguishable for several yards around.
Dogs by the noise have been shied to alleys,
And the whole street is citizen against glass.
The barber comes out of his shop, hands on hips
And apron littered with the hair of a customer
Slow to get out of the chair to see the attraction.
He takes a hit full to the chest, ricochets
Off his shop's doorframe, falls on the macadam
Dead as our tourist trade in fall. Step by step
The man begins down the street and doors open,
Merchants and customers coming out to see the commotion.
A boy leaning out a second story window is caught
Almost flush in the forehead and that window frame
Will need be painted, if not sanded as well.
The man reloads with the economical moves of an expert,
Sways in his walk with a self-assurance
We haven't seen for years. You can see

Without knowing what he is doing that he knows
What he is doing. A small child at point blank range
After the shot is not well recognized as boy or girl.
Patrons of restaurants bring their meals in cupped arms
Onto the sidewalk. The pistol smokes and arches
With each explosion in the man's hands.
No law of physics is too small, no act
Of chemistry overlooked.
This can be no ordinary day.

SECOND CLASS CITIZEN

I was told it had something to do
With the pulling out of the right combination,
The precise staircase of molecules, inserting it
Into something as ordinary as bacteria -
And letting that bacteria, in making itself,
Make that combination over and over and over.
First it was the cleansing of defect, and I welcomed that.
Then new crops, and I had to get on the bandwagon
Or the prices would fall. We had such yields
I wondered if you could do the same thing
To the house, halve my chores, get a little order
Out of this clutter. Of course not. Then
The stock - the strong, alert young
Brought in by truck, growing almost
To twice the normal animal's size, and seeming
To eat no more. A man with six old-issue cows,
Fields larger hardly than a garden, could never
Keep up, would be run out and the land bought
For someone with new ideas. I look at our
Huge stock, know the guarantee on the traits
Breeding true, wonder how tough the meat will be.
The will to stay quiet in the pen engineered
Right in to them, I didn't have to
As first suspected reinforce fences, close off
The porch. In shear poundage, meat
And grain, we are producing perhaps
Twice as much with but
An equal overall cost. Prices go down.
We move more out, take the same in.
We send our daughter out on her date

In a dress left over from your Aunt Edna,
Have to pool our allowances to fill her make-up kit.
You invite the boy when he comes for her
Into our off-center living room, have him sit
On the end of the couch with the sink.
He ducks his head slightly through the door,
Walks softly around a poorly placed chair,
Drops gracile fingers over the sofa arm.
Every ounce of his body is in position,
Each movement correctly follows the one before;
Gravity gives him his weight; his clothes
Suit him better than my skin suits me.
His voice is exact pitch, precision cut.
You know what he's taking our daughter out for.
Why make it worse for her,
Why ask him whose son he is?

THE SON

I waited for the train half a day,
Made a nuisance of myself at the ticket window.
An hour late the engine burred in,
Lugubrious and squat on the tracks,
Its board advertising spotted so badly
I could hardly read the half of it.
But his poster was there. Elephants
And a huge, red, useless ball in the background;
He bent back in a bathing suit and opened his mouth
To a stone in his hand the size of a pebble.
Placards for the rubberman, the lion tamer
And the gorilla woman were larger.
Even the horseback riders got better billing.
At first, a dozen workmen stumbled out,
Kept onlookers back and set to unloading the animals,
And for all I know he could have been
Among them. Slowly, the body of performers
In drab and business suits filed off,
Avoiding those few who leaned from the platform to watch;
I have my hopes he was with those. We need
Gather a number of smaller stones,
Bring nothing larger than will fit a hand.
My child, the stone eater. Your purse we can
Fill to the clasp; if you get tired
With holding it, the public can be damned
And I'll carry the bag. My coat with the extra weight
Is coming apart at the shoulders and our yard
Is pocked with the loss of rock. He is
Our only son; I want to see
If he has in truth made something of himself.

HOW THE CHILDREN ARE RAISED

We cannot take another child.
Four already, and we did not want any.
The youngest is barely to the stage
Where a man can sleep all night.
Toys from the older ones make it impossible
To walk the house at night, to cut the lawn
Without clearing streak by streak a path.
The neighborhood is full with children.
Front yards all day are coveys of young
Drifting with the calls of older children, parents.
No one has the resources to properly raise children,
But when the hospital calls and says
One has come out of the incubator
Just for you, there is no refusing.
You draw in the bottom of your breath,
Obey the law, go down and ask
Which one. Once home, they all get mixed up. The neighbors'
All-of-one-face children mingle with yours
And the object is to collect the proper number
Of small, quiet, light eaters. Children learn
New names, new addresses; learn that the simple
And inexpensive can demand other perks.
But a loud, self-aggrandized infant is hard to switch.
With a good newborn parents keep the child inside,
Are suspicious of everyone coming to the door.
Hopefully, this one will be the last.
The wife in the pantry readies linen, and the children
In the living room plot games against the innocent.

They tremble of duty, their father's one way with the world,
Their mother's resilience and replaceability.
I am the occupant, the citizen. I find the car keys,
Go get the undeserved bastard.

PRIVATE ACTS

He's been out all morning, missed
Breakfast, forgotten he has today to go to school.
Our two other boys are good to take up
His chores, but I don't think
He should be let out of his fair share.
Added to it, he's made a mess the family
Will spend hours to clean up. I want to give him
All the chance I can for him to make even,
To break out his talent, unfold it
And make it solid. But one of his prodigies already
Has run through your pantry, in sheer joy
Turned over last year's preserves.
When they come out of the ground they
Take to running and leaping and stumbling and
Breaking limbs, or stand with that look
That has caused me to lock our two daughters
In their room, load the shotgun,
Put out the boy's baseball bat. Reading
Does this to a man. Had he been content
With house opinions, settled with the ordinary,
He'd have been a practical child, set his lessons out
Like machine work, worried more
The side of the land he could see.
Half a dozen of the ones he's raised latest
Dance around him in a quarter circle
And a man who buys land next to a graveyard
Is a fool. I had no foresight.
He claps and shimmies and cants runes
And another comes up and he's going to miss
All day at school. We'll never get him
To sit quietly to supper, keep him from crawling

Out on the roof and down the gutter to raise
More, people our whole place with the dead.
I need all my sons to keep this home going.
He stands as strong as Goliath, pulling them out
Without thought, without plan, calling them up.
Think of something. I'll admit it's what I get
For marrying a wench. He's your fault
And don't think, the time come, I'll plant you
In a place the boy with all his art will ever find.

REVIVAL

The pumpkins burst into flame.
The man raises both hands, eyes closed.
The corn whips one way, bows the other.
String beans burst into bloom.
He turns his face to the top of the tent
And lets go his words. Hogs
And cattle speak, snakes stand on their tails.
Ordinary people feel themselves lifted
Out of the integument, torn
Into new space. The earth
Has eight dimensions, or ten. The clouds
Race into each other, or race away. Surely
The minister will get with the McClellan girl
A lot farther than the rest - who,
It is rumored, got well into a laying on
Of hands, but could convince her no further.
Rains fall out of clear air, and common
House pets babble in tongues. A Friday night
And no one would be here. Thursdays
Always bring out the best crowds, the week
Almost over but the weariness bought in weekends
Not yet in the bone. Arthritis disappears
And cataracts reverse. The McClellan girl
Stands in a body that could make Adam sin.
We clap, we sing. The late sun
Stands still and is passed by the moon.
The minister grins like a drunk in a whorehouse.
We grin back, our fishnet stockings tight to the thigh,
Our lipstick redder than the wounds of Christ.
The McClellan girl sings, but too loudly.

THE COMMON

They were the best of neighbors. No one doubted
We could get the place up in the air,
Could actually put the house on clouds,
Hold it stable with a foundation of oxygen,
Dust, water vapor and whatnot. Friends praised
The good sense in putting it all together on the ground,
Fixing boards and windows and even the fence -
Came by in ones and twos to help, would not question
Our plan to one day set it up,
Level the finished structure half a mile in clear nothing.
Failing to first move in the furniture was the worst of it.
The pulley we had rigged far too small
For sofas and beds, we had to modify,
Get four men on the ground to hoist our belongings up -
And the furniture in, we had to level it,
Counterbalance everything, get slowly the whole of our possessions
Screwed into place. But no one disbelieved.
Our guests weren't the least bit afraid,
Climbed out of the hand-rope elevator, commented
The beauty of mere cubic space, said they had heard
That to watch a thunderstorm from here
Was the same as the grace of measuring God's windows. Simple
    farmers
I'd have thought they would challenge the physics,
Deny the motives, try to pull us down with wires.
Every so often someone will come just to sit, acts
As though we have by settling here
Done them all some great, personal favor.
On the porch I talk with an architect,
Planning for a cottage to go up in addition,
And his amazement is only the sight of birds

Flying under us. We light cigars, watch the smoke
Swirl off the edge of the stoop, downward.
I yell at our youngest son again forgetting,
Stepping almost off the edge of the porch; and the man,
Without breath as the boy stumbles back to safety,
Says *Yes, yes, I can build you a house.*

THE TRANSMISSION OF IDEAS

Though you usually find it only in fools,
The deformed and the half-witted, he has the gift.
He can sit on his back porch
And summon the birds. Garden snakes
Will come out to sun at his feet.
The meanest dog in the county will go silent
At his attention. A bobcat, spawning a litter
Under his front stoop, will not stir
When he reaches in for the young.
There is something in the rhythm of his walk,
Or in the paper flutter of his eyes.
Around him it is hard not to watch for the secret,
To observe him as high-school boys would
The one boy who seems to have the way with women.
Perhaps there is some sound he silently makes,
A twisting of the shoulders and head,
A suturing of the breath. Occasionally
A deer will walk right through his garden,
Lay its head in his lap. I think
There is a magnetism about him, a flinging out
Of character, a sheer dominance of personality.
His table is always stacked with meat,
And he makes the best stews around. Often
He takes more than he can keep, too much in
The joy of it, and the neighbors benefit.
The prey will walk easily into his hands
And with his hands alone he makes the kill. His palms
For days stink of it. For the rest of us
Our only innocents are the wife and children,
Our palms are the smell of the moon. He calls

Into his small backyard an eight-point buck
And with his freezer full many of us will have deer meat.
We begin to admire the strength of his arms,
The width of his back. We begin to exercise
Our own ordinary, purposeless muscles.
We learn, perform as best we can
Against the poor material we have within reach.

THE DOCTOR

The village rises to its haunches.
A thousand fires burst to life in every window.
Huge bells and clock chimes begin to sound.
First, at the edge of town, are men with torches.
Just behind, children peer between adult knees.
At the last, women wait in ambush.
Immense dancings. The mayor takes my hand.
We go round and round: the torches are piled
In one huge, Sunday bonfire. A shopkeeper
Advances to offer his daughter as sacrifice,
His knife quivering breaths above her chest.
How can I refuse with grace? Children
Grab at my pants' legs. A dog
Is split down the middle, his bowels
Tossed steaming on the fire.
I am given the bailiff's wife.
Someone holds a baby out to me
To apportion as I please. I open my black bag
And wave all manner of silver instrument in the air.

THE PROPHET WHO WOULD PROVE THE REAL AND EVERYDAY EXISTENCE OF GOD

A few have put on their Sunday best.
Most show up in work-clothes, their time
Taken from the garden or kitchen. One woman
Has brought a folding chair, and her knitting.
A few gaze extraordinarily up, but most eye
The Prophet. Eleven fifteen of a morning
Is a damned inconvenient time to prove the existence of God.
A few parents have kept their children out of school,
But the classrooms hardly miss them. A young couple,
Credulous and with little to lose, hold each other
More in fear of their past than of this event.
At eleven fifteen men are already thinking how much
They've wasted, how far now they are
From where they should be. Children playing
Cannot be quieted, and the knitting woman
For the second folds her hands in her lap.
Above, two crows sit on the telephone wire.
The Prophet holds his hands wide apart,
Turns up his face and drums out a prayer
That could convince even half deities of ill repute
That this man means no harm.
One of the crows spreads full his colossal wings
And drifts from the line, spinning out over the fields
And into a shaft of warm air,
Rising, rising…

HATING THE CRAFTSMAN

This has been the goddamnedest ice storm
I've seen. An hour and all the power lines were down.
I sat out on the porch, my winter coat
And straight bourbon, listening
To trees crack, the shattering of ice
And bark as limbs hit ground.
In the driveway the car was cemented in place.
Farley used a cigarette lighter, bored
A hole into the door for his car key,
Couldn't budge the door once it was unlocked.
Windows all along the street are submerged
In four to six inches of frozen water.
Some idiot had clothes on the line and now
Sheets are walls, shirts hardly sway,
Underthings are the cores of mere brick.
I don't think much of it when I see
The first child frozen on his tricycle.
His parents should have never let him out.
A woman races in a bathing suit through the ice,
Runs laughing to a neighbor's porch.
I slide down in my coat, sweat causing the down
To stick to my arms, my hair to flatten at the collar.
July wind beats around the house corner,
Ice closes the spaces in the balustrade.
I can hear you knocking on the living room pane.
Out in the yard birds are frozen to our grass,
Dim centers to ice mounds. Yet
Anything at flight still flies,
Anything defying common sense goes on.
I can hear you banging on the glass,

Waving me in. You know once more
As in the past three early summer ice storms
I'll hook up the hose at the back faucet,
Try for ice and come up with water.
I'd love to please you this year more than anything.
A man holds his hand in the freezing rain
Long enough for it to be well coated,
Draws it back under an eave. The bastard
Thinks he's done something. Against all
The best wishes of us both, I go for that hose.

COMBUSTIBLE

The man on fire wanders about mostly at night.
He knows he is a spectacular sight at any time,
But at night he can be seen farther, cast his coming
Around the edges of barns, reflect off the Sound
Occasionally for miles. During the day he is
An eyeful too; but after dark children
Will crouch on their knees in bed to watch
Through their windows for the burning man to cross a yard.
Young boys use him as an excuse to get
Girls who wish to stay away from outright agreement
To drive with them to the black backs of fields,
Or down roads whose abrupt ends have been for years
Welcomed. He knows he is nothing if he is too common,
Restricts himself to just so much wandering
As will make the sight of him plausible
And rare enough to be worth the drive.
Most adults by now have come to the opinion
That the man on fire enjoys his status,
Has long since stopped thinking of how his condition
Might for his own good be put to an end.
Not many people remember what he was before
He caught fire, what his habits were, whether
He could get credit with only his word and
A right hand. When he talks to neighbors
Now it is only at distance, and by shouting, and only
Of the common information a few words in their roughest form
Can edge through wonderment or bother.
He is, in himself, still a slow sort,
Proud to be out of the crowd in his burning,
Taking the attention for as long a ride

As a man without commercial backing can get.
No one hereabouts would want him, burning
Or otherwise, to ask a daughter out, even
If she were past good dating age and worn with use.
But his burning still for everyone is thrill,
And the locals talk of him to tourists like even tourist
Should know that behind such good the purpose is clear.

FREEDOM

Waiting children wear bright reds and yellows.
Their parents in gray at the sides of the street
Remain still, but believe yet their children
Might whirl loose in the air, hold each other
With only fingertips, breed agility and metrics.
Adults shuffle their black shoes, bend at the necks
Like button hooks, pull collars close
And think that the dust does not, to begin with,
Mean harm. One child
Has three feathers stuck in the back of her hair;
Another uses bows in place of buttons. A boy
With braids holds his arms finger length from his side
To preserve longer his family's week's pay worth of satin.
The sun seems on purpose twice as strong as usual.
When the man comes out of his new shop,
Parting the crowd with the backs of his hands,
Some children spin, leap to one leg.
A boy does the tucked double flip
His uncle has assured him will make
For courting days short on preliminaries.
In the street the man edges a square from the crowd,
Unfolding a gray cloth colored with black boot prints,
White numbers. Arms stiff
As the handles of teakettles, light on his toes
As though the man might worry of breaking his own feet, he steps
First one set of numbers straight through,
And then another. Parents shift forward,
Their faces common angles and their shoulders flattened,
As their children quiet and begin to look down
Cautiously at the gray cloth. The man

Steps through the boot prints in numerical order
Again, and bows. His smile is a salesman's.
For loved children this will not be enough.
A father places his feet in one pair
Of thin black boot prints, his face
Going blood and his breathing shallow;
A child not his own pulls in question
At his pants leg. This does
No one any good. A woman unwraps the rainbow shawl
From her daughter's otherwise bare shoulders,
Stuffs all of it deep within a coat pocket,
Advances on the man with one quivering finger raised.
The man steps his prints, chin out,
His black cuffs drunk, his heels like spiders in a fire.

THE CRASHED SPACE TRAVELLER IN MCCLELLAN'S BASEMENT

No one talks to him when he's in his gaseous state.
He rolls red and blue and the ends of his nerves
Grate along the glass of his home like wire
On the skin. You must wait.
In an hour or so he flashes back to liquid,
Begins at the edges to turn solid
And then you can reason. When he is solid
He does not hear. Our pops and squeaks are not
All that compatible. That he knows the language at all
Sometimes seems large enough accomplishment.
He whines in a deep yellow voice and for the cry
He lets out when I turn off the basement light
I think he eats his energy raw, has an appetite
Bigger than a man could support with summer rates on the electric.
He seems amiable enough when neighbors drop by,
Whipping around in his cube like the ghost of a lively man.
If there are enough people he'll go
Gaseous to liquid to stone thick solid
And back to each sometimes twice or more.
The local lads love it, and half a dozen
Want him for their science projects.
I won't let him leave the basement, though.
His ship in thousands of pieces forty feet deep in the muck,
All he could hope for was a basement almost warm,
Someone now and again to turn on the light.
Still, anger does rise up in him and he shows
He has learned the language my wife prays
I haven't taught the children. Sometimes
To shut him up I have to tap on the glass,

Even occasionally bring down the hammer,
Snap the wooden end against the cube's face he's closest to.
The glass seems an ordinary glass,
One that a man with a good arm
Could in one swing break. He and I
Both understand that one day there will be a crack,
And then a full roundhouse that lets the atmosphere out.
In a world like this the days line up for it.
Until then, the show is all for you.

THE MAN WHO CARVED HIS WIFE'S HEART

When he first brought it home as a block of wood
His wife said *Only on the porch;* and, for the most part,
That is where he carved. Occasionally
He would carry it down to Henson's store
And sit in the rotting, no-reclining recliner,
Working in half inch nicks -
One knife blade only, and that folding.
Seasons ago Henson would sell his carvings
For fifty percent off the top; but
An extra rack of coke does better,
And sometimes it is two months
Before life comes to a carving. In the past
His wife would let him sit at the kitchen table,
The shavings below him caught on newspaper.
This time she points to the wooden chair
Outdoors, leaves him the broom. But at night
He brings his work in and places it on the dresser
Where she can hear it night after night coming out of the wood -
One chamber pumping, then weeks later another,
Valves pattering like the children of arithmetic.
He puts it under an arm, carries it with him. She sees it
As an object he palms, worth to a tourist six dollars,
Years left on a mantle, and one day in the fire.
At her table only birds, a stoat, foxes
And mice, a clatter in the cabinet
And then out of sight.

THE PRAGMATIST

Split rail and white picket. Privacy
And redwood. Plank and stone.
Barbed wire. Around the house.
All along the road. By the shore line.
On both sides of the drain-ditches,
Protection. I've got nothing else to do.
You can't hire workmen worth half their price.
Tools are simple: post-hole diggers,
Hammer and nail, maul and saw. The ground
Is sainted with water, you can drive
A post most times without digging,
Taking that you don't expect it to last
Forever. A dozen good storms,
A few good Carolina, or even Virginia, boys
Racing through the field drunk and turning away
Just one moment before clipping it dead on - or
The fishermen, using it as support for crossing
The ditches, or resting place when, novices,
They carry too much with them from their car
At the side of the Refuge road -
And it will be turned over, pulling maybe
The rest with it, starting a whole strip
Of fence to lay over. The wood or link
You can most often simply salvage, back up
To a falling down place and carefully
Move out what you want. Chain link,
Posts, in Norfolk you can buy as seconds,
Haul them out here in a flatbed. The posts
Up by the house I pack in with concrete,
The planks or link I put solidly down.

The wife uses one high fence as a clothesline.
I lean across a particularly low stretch
Of oak and four inch square stanchions,
Waiting for the sun to die and drinking iced tea.
My daughter racing through the twists
Of boards and metal often gives up
And where she can climbs over. The wife
Makes more tea, brings it out in large glasses.
And I worry about the heat, the garden, the drying
Of clothes, her tan like a slaver's chattel-mark.

THE MULE

What they could do they did. Two years
Almost every day the talk was of what
To do about it, thoughts being smashed together
And their electricity swept under the kitchen table.
A few local remedies seemed for a few days
To work, but piece by piece still
Their daughter would change and one day
The last of it came over and the daughter
Was a mule. For a time they tried
To hold the condition as changeable, would have
No doubt, if the girl's room had not been
On the second floor, left her there,
Pretended perhaps for as long as it might take
That nothing had happened. A month
They housed her downstairs, but the furniture
No matter how it was set was always
In the many wrong places, chairs looking
For a rear hoof and the doorways misplaced.
The back of the barn was painted pink,
Stuffed animals, wall posters and the phonograph
Brought down from her old room - but even then
The feeding, hygiene and everyday upkeep
Fit a mule better than a daughter, and the family
As well as the neighbors could see the outcome.
Farms these days are machinery and news
Of a mule in a man's barn travels.
Not long and the McClellan boys will sneak
Half-drunk in and take her for a ride,
With the sheriff calling next morning
Her father to say come get your mule,

It's loose on the courthouse lawn.
The pink paint will not be renewed.
Stuffed animals, phonograph will go out
To the trash as they variously get in the way.
The parents will think less of the girl, more
Of the mule, come to terms of it and not she.
One day another man will come into the kitchen
And note the family has no use for a mule
On this land, and offer pleasantly to take the animal
Away, even pay a little for it. If not
With this man, with one of the next
A deal will be made. No questions asked.
What can be done and what can't
And a slap on the animal's rump as it is led
Easily, perhaps in a numb, happy quickness, away.

THE ROMANCE OF A NONBELIEVER

When he raises the dead grown men cry
My wife assures me. I've checked twice,
But no money has changed hands. Not that I would mind
Paying more for the show - but only where the wife
Might laugh as well, get at least a good night's
Good sense out of it. Serious as a week's rain
After a week's rain, she intends with two
Other couples this put on to be real. I know
The man does it for free only as
A teaser, will soon be bringing back loved ones
At fifty cents a word, fifty dollars a rap
On the table, maybe as mist in the kitchen
For two hundred. Like me, the other husbands
Are coming to find the wires and foot treadles,
Point out how commonplace anything the dead say
Through our medium is. I expect him
To seat the wives, treat them like they were still of a state
To dance topless at bar for tips alone.
No doubt he will have a full black coat, a voice
That makes good people think of an older man
Watching children run on a playground.
His movements will be as slow as the wife
After ten years in bed even when her flannel nightgown
Isn't in the way. I've seen all
The Christopher Lee and Peter Cushing movies:
I'll know if he moves the table with his knees.
But when he gooses my wife and claims the dead know
She was in a former life the wife of a passionate man
That is when I go over the top
And we get all of this set down to basics.

THE LAST STAND OF THE BIRDWOMEN

They cling to the sides of buildings. People below
Wave from a broad measure out in towards
Their chests: *Come down*. They flock
Above one of the highest structures,
Circle to ledges, toy with flagpoles
And antennas and support wires.
Building attendants try to reach them, bring up ladders,
Lean almost too far. A mother complains
That they fly naked, rushes her two boys
Under the cover of a rain protection at a bus stop.
They twist in the hot currents of ceiling exhausts,
Make delicate spins away from certain collision.
Some of the spectators stare in awe,
Others think the aerialists too proud;
The talk is mixed of acrobatic acumen
And of salacious respect for the bodies.
Business men crowd the windows. One stretches
Her wings to a full twelve-foot length,
Roars in the air, sends onlookers
Crashing back. A boy, with neither
Wonder nor prurient thoughts, points,
Picks a small, still one out
And finds a stone in the street.
Striking, gauze skin giving way, hollow bone
Bursting, he thinks: how fragile
They are, how easily bent, how readily drawn common.
From the useless, damaged wings she pulls herself free
And angrily the woman comes down.

www.ingramcontent.com/pod-product-compliance
Lightning Source LLC
LaVergne TN
LVHW011215080426
835508LV00007B/793